Acknowledgements
The author, photographer and publisher would like to thank
Mr and Mrs Shanti Prakash Das and Bublee, without whose
help this book would not have been possible.

British Library Cataloguing in Publication Data
Mathieson, Feroza
    The very special sari.
    I. Title   II. Das, Prodeepta   III. Series
823'.914[J]
ISBN 0-7136-3064-7

© 1988 A & C Black (Publishers) Limited

Published by A & C Black (Publishers) Ltd
35 Bedford Row, London WC1R 4JH

All rights reserved. No part of this publication
may be reproduced, stored in a retrieval system,
or transmitted in any form or by any means, electronic,
mechanical, photocopying or otherwise without the prior
permission of A & C Black (Publishers) Limited

Filmset by August Filmsetting, Haydock, St Helens
Printed in Belgium by Henri Proost & Cie Pvba

The Very Special Sari

Feroza Mathieson

Photographs by Prodeepta Das

A & C Black · London

Mum and Dad had an invitation to a wedding party. It would be a very big party with lots of people dressed up in their best clothes.

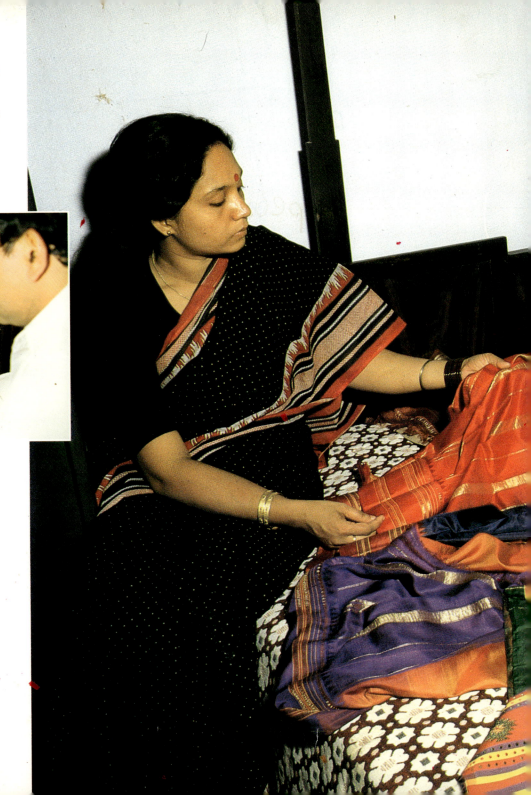

'I'll have to wear something extra special,' said Mum. She got out all her saris, but none of them seemed quite right.

'We'll buy some material,' said Mum. 'And I'll ask Mrs Nayak to make me something new.'

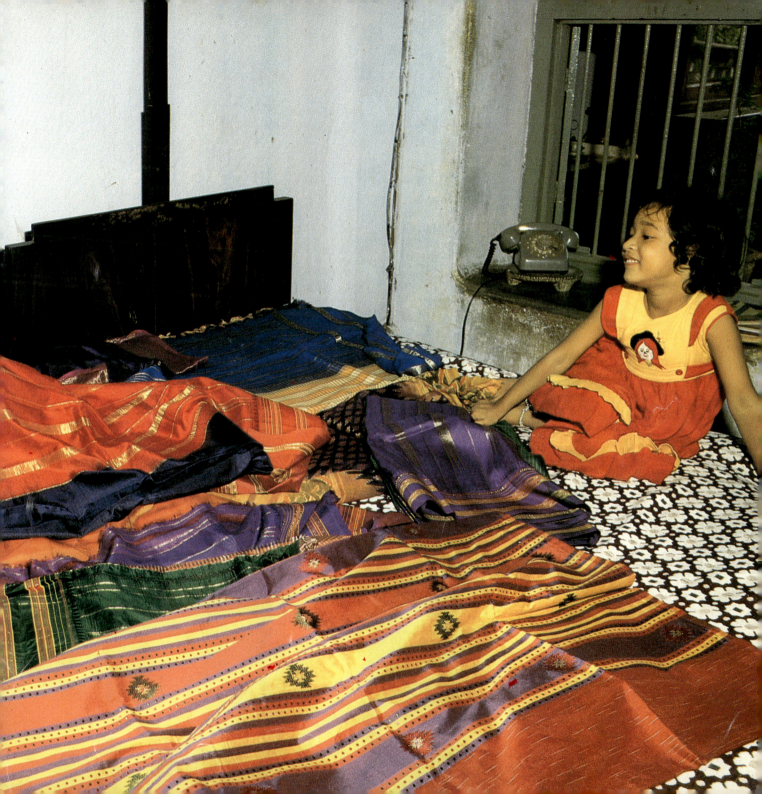

The next day, Gita and her mum set off to buy all the things they would need: material, beads, thread, sequins and mirrors.

First they went to the material shop.

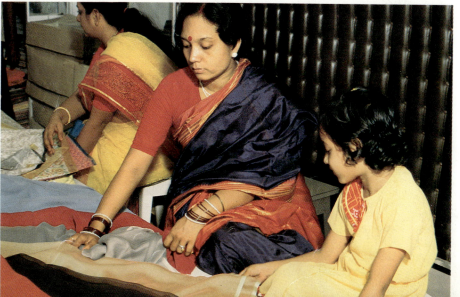

There was a lot of material to choose from.

Gita helped Mum to choose some red material that was as soft as silk.

'Oh, how pretty,' said Gita.
'Yes, it's going to be a beautiful sari when it's finished,' said Mum.

The shopkeeper cut a big piece of material for them. 'I wish I was having a new outfit too,' thought Gita.

Next they went to buy the beads. There were lots and lots to choose from, in all different colours.

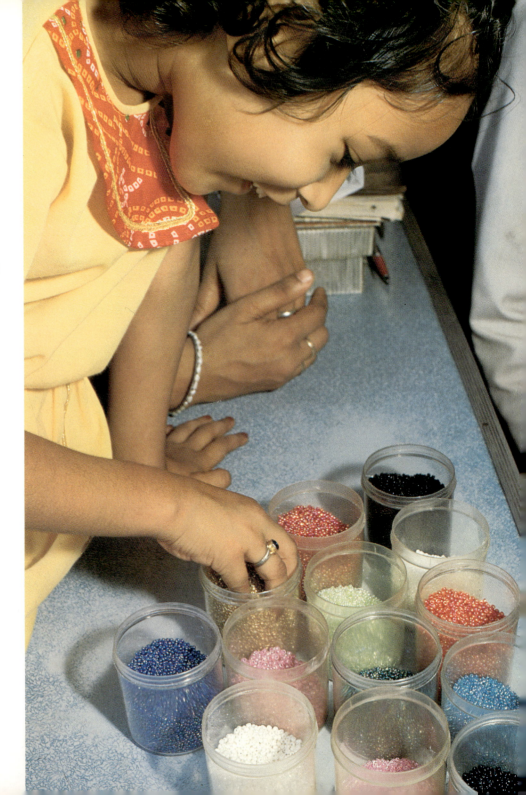

Mum chose white ones, and the shopkeeper weighed them on his scales.

'Oh, how pretty,' said Gita.

'Yes, it's going to be a beautiful sari when it's finished,' said Mum.

'I wish I was having a new suit too,' thought Gita.

'Now we need some thread,' said Mum.

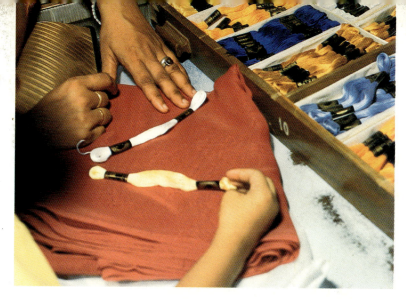

'Shall we have yellow, or maybe white?'

No, gold and silver looked best, so that's what they chose.
One of silver and one of gold.

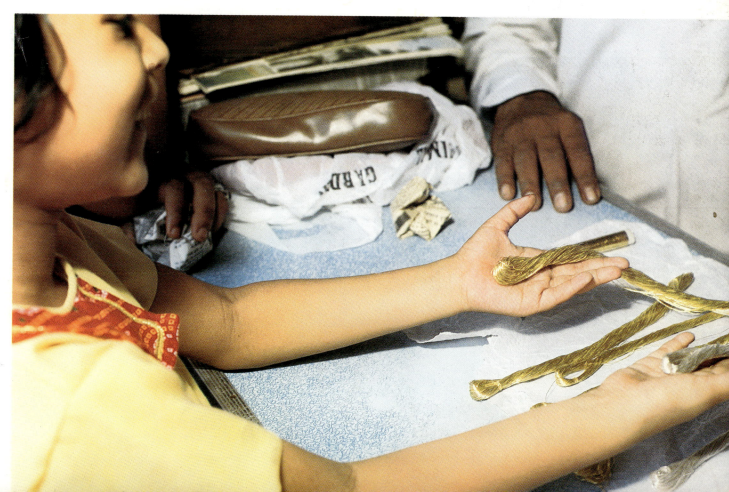

'What's next?' said Mum.

'Mirrors and sequins,' said Gita. 'To make your sari sparkle.'

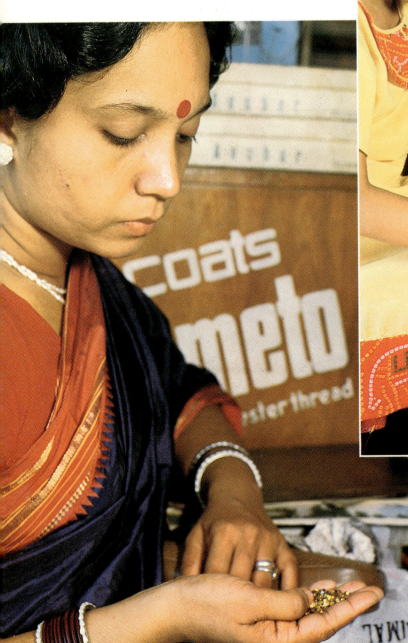

Mum chose some gold sequins.

'Can we have some of these?' said Gita. In each tiny mirror she could see her face. Mum bought a boxful and paid the shopkeeper.

'How pretty the sari is going to be,' thought Gita. 'I wish I could have one too.'

Now all they had to do was take everything to Mrs Nayak's shop.

Mum sat down and told Mrs Nayak how she wanted the beads and sequins to be sewn.

While Mum talked, Gita stared at all the beautiful clothes in the shop. 'I wish I could have some new clothes too,' she thought.

The sari would be ready in one week.
Gita couldn't wait to see it.

All week, she thought about the new sari.
Mum already had lots of splendid saris,
but this one would be extra special.

Gita wished she could wear a new outfit and go to the wedding. Everyone would say she looked beautiful.

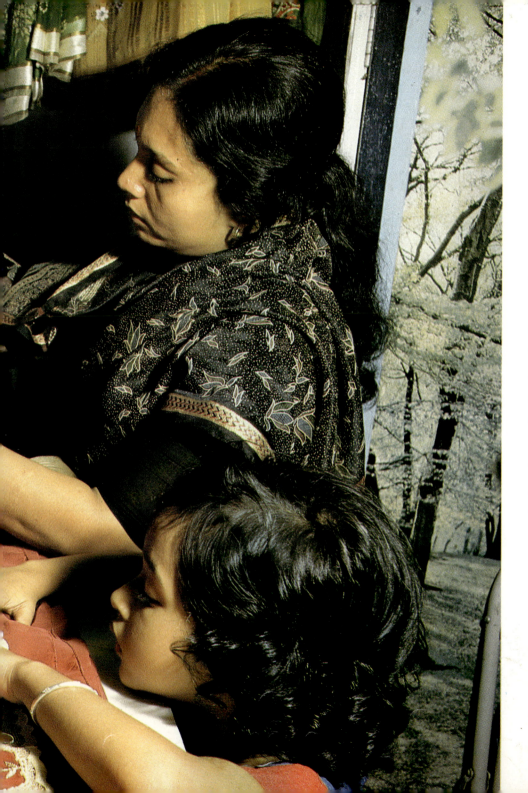

Well, the day came when they went to collect the sari. Gita couldn't believe her eyes. It was magnificent. Mum was going to look lovely.

What a pity Gita couldn't go to the wedding.

Mrs Nayak folded the sari and gave it to Mum.

Then she took a parcel out of the cupboard and Mum quickly put it into her bag.

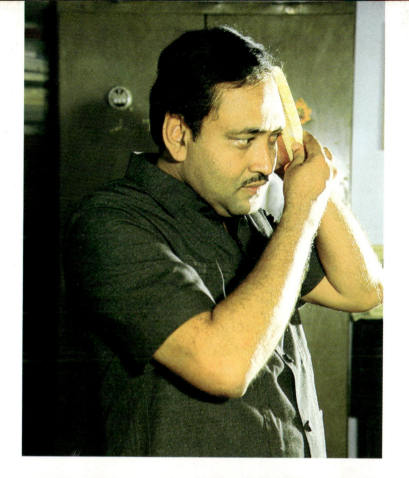

The next day, Mum and Dad began to get ready for the wedding.

Aunty Sita was going to come and look after Gita for the day, but Gita didn't want to stay at home. She wanted to go to the wedding.

'When will Aunty Sita be here?' asked Gita.

'Oh, didn't I tell you?' said Mum. 'Aunty Sita can't come today, so it looks as though you'll have to come with us.'

'But what am I going to wear?' asked Gita excitedly.

'Go and look in your cupboard,' said Mum. 'There must be something in there.'

Gita ran to her bedroom and opened the cupboard. What do you think she saw? It was a beautiful new shalwaar chemise in her favourite colour – pink!

So Gita did get a new outfit after all, and she was going to the wedding. She was so happy, she gave Mum and Dad a big hug.

'How ever did you get it made without me knowing?' she said. Mum and Dad looked at each other and laughed.